THE EFFORTLESS SOUS VIDE COOKBOOK
For Beginners

Easy, Quick, and Foolproof Recipes for Crafting Restaurant-Quality Meals Every Day.

Sophia Marchesi

IPPOCERONTE
publishing

**Copyright © 2021 by Sophia Marchesi
All rights reserved**

This document is geared towards providing exact and reliable information with regards to the topic and issue covered. The publication is sold with the idea that the publisher is not required to render accounting, officially permitted, or otherwise, qualified services. If advice is necessary, legal or professional, a practiced individual in the profession should be ordered.

From a Declaration of Principles which was accepted and approved equally by a Committee of the American Bar Association and a Committee of Publishers and Associations.

In no way is it legal to reproduce, duplicate, or transmit any part of this document in either electronic means or in printed format. Recording of this publication is strictly prohibited and any storage of this document is not allowed unless with the written permission from the publisher. All rights reserved.

The information provided herein is stated to be truthful and consistent, in that liability, in terms of inattention or otherwise, by any usage or abuse of any policies, processes, or directions contained within is the solitary and utter responsibility of the recipient reader. Under no circumstances will any legal responsibility or blame be held against the publisher for any reparation, damages, or monetary loss due to the information herein, either directly or indirectly.

Respective authors own all copyrights not held by the publisher.

The information herein is offered for informational purposes solely and is universal as so. The presentation of the information is without a contract or any type of guarantee assurance.

The trademarks that are used are without any consent, and the publication of the trademark is without permission or backing by the trademark owner. All trademarks and brands within this book are for clarifying purposes only and are owned by the owners themselves, not affiliated with this document.

CONTENTS

INTRODUCTION 7
RECIPES 11
1. Bolognese Sauce for Spaghetti 12
2. Shrimp Soup 14
3. Omelet With Parmesan 16
4. Chocolate Chip Cookies 18
5. Lemon Curd 20
6. Sweet Plums 22
7. Creamy Tomato Soup 24
8. Olives Squash 26
9. Mushrooms 28
10. Hard-Boiled Eggs 30
11. Breakfast Yogurt 31
12. Tangy Garlic Chili Tofu 32
13. Hanger Steak 34
14. Amazing Chicken 36
15. Simple Rack of Lamb 38
16. Pork Carnitas 40
17. Speedy Poached Tomatoes 42
18. Buffalo Chicken Wings 44
19. Szechuan Broccoli 46
20. Mashed Potatoes 48
21. Scallops with Brown Butter 50
22. Swordfish 52
23. Persimmon Butter Toasts 54
24. Tender Pork Chops 56
25. Holiday Cranberry Sauce 58
26. Juicy Beer-Infused Sausages 60

27. Chicken and Vegetable Soup 62
28. Creamy Cauliflower Broccoli Soup 64
29. Teriyaki Salmon 66
30. Strawberries 68
31. Mixed Vegetables 70
32. Sweet Potato Fries 72
33. Scrambled Eggs 74
34. Harissa Chicken 76
35. Apple Butternut Squash Soup 78
36. Walnut Coated Halibut 80
37. Spicy Butter Poached Asparagus 82
38. Fudgy Brownies 84
39. Cold Pea and Yogurt Soup 86
40. Power Green Soup 88
41. Bacon Brussels Sprouts 90
42. Trout 91
43. Fennel Risotto 92
44. Sesame Eggplant 94
45. Crème Brulée with Blueberries 96
46. Kale Cheese 98
47. Red Wine Poached Pears 100
48. Buttered Spiced Apples 102
49. Blueberry Jam 104
50. Artichoke 106
TEMPERATURE CHARTS 108
COOKING CONVERSION 114
RECIPE INDEX 118

INTRODUCTION

Cooking is something that runs in my blood, most of my food memories are of my Nan cooking Sunday dinners - lasagna and cannelloni to share with the whole family. When I was young, I have never liked to be stuck in a classroom, I started culinary school at a very young age, and the only thing I really wanted was to be out cooking. You could say I was not a particularly good student, but I have always been really passionate about food.

I have been working in a professional kitchen since I was seventeen years old and I'm running my own restaurant since I was 23. The past thirty years have been a rewarding, yet arduous journey that I spent learning the basics and mastering the different cuisines and techniques by taking the best out of each of them. It was last year, during the lockdown, that I realized that I was starting to lose my passion. Preparing a dish had become an aseptic and mechanical where perfection was king.

I wanted to go back to my roots, cooking has always been about my family; preparing a dish together with the people I love gives me time to connect and create precious memories. Setting aside a time where the entire family can work together to create a meal gives us a chance to pause, catch up and just connect with each other.

What I would like to share with you in this book is my renewed passion and a technique that I learned during my time in France, the Sous Vide. This innovative cooking method is something my grandmother never thought existed and creates the perfect opportunity to spend some time in the kitchen with my family. For these reasons, I think the Sous Vide is the perfect combination of my professional and domestic life.

Sous Vide is the French term that translates to "under vacuum" and it is the method for preparing a dish at a specifically controlled temperature and time; your food should be prepared at the temperature at which it will be eaten. Put simply, this procedure involves placing food in vacuum seal bags and boiling it in a specially built bath of water for longer than average cooking times (usually 1 to 7 hours, up to 48 or more in some cases). Cooking at an exact temperature takes the guesswork out of the equation that defines a perfect meal. You can easily prepare your steak, chicken, lamb, pork, etc., exactly the way you like it, every single time.

It is easy to use and leads to great results every time. You will end up with food that is more tender and juicier than anything else you've ever made. This technique will help you to take your everyday cooking to a higher level. To do a top dish, most of the time, you do not need exotic ingredients, it is just a matter to get the best from the ingredients you already know.

The greatest part of Sous Vide cooking is that it does not require your constant presence in the kitchen. When the food is sealed in a bag and placed in the water bath, you can leave it at a low temperature, and it will cook on its own without asking much of your attention. The Sous Vide Cookers that are nowadays available in the market are efficient at regulating the perfect temperature to cook food according to its texture while maintaining the minimum required temperature. So, while your food is in the water, your hands are practically free to work on other important tasks or spend some quality time with your family.

It is an artful skill that is definitely worth trying. If it is just your first time, don't feel bad if you don't get the results you wanted to achieve. You will get better by gaining experience with this cookbook! The key is having patience, the right information, and consistency.

The meals prepared with Sous Vide are tasty and healthy, since this technique does not use added fats during the preparation of your dish also, using low temperature ensures that the perfect cooking point is reached.

Dishes included in this cookbook are simple, delicious, and provide you with so many options that you'll be preparing them for years to come. These recipes are made to be shared with the people you love and to build new precious food memories as I did with my Nan.

RECIPES

1. BOLOGNESE SAUCE FOR SPAGHETTI

Cal.: 424 | Fat: 29g | Protein: 14g

Preparation Time: 8 minutes
Cooking Time: 3 hours
Servings: 4

Photo by Klaus Nielsen from Pexels

Ingredients

250 g ground beef
1 garlic clove
1 onion
300 g tomato purée
1 tbsp. rapeseed oil
1 teaspoon dried basil
½ teaspoon chili flakes
1 tablespoon sugar
Salt

Directions

1. Preheat the water bath to 162°F/72°C.

2. Mix tomato purée and minced meat in a bowl with sugar, basil, chili flakes and 1 teaspoon of salt to form a smooth sauce.

3. Sauté onion cubes and finely chopped garlic clove in hot oil until golden brown. Add to the mince mixture and stir.

4. Divide the sauce between two bags and vacuum seal. Cook for 2 hours and 40 minutes in a water bath.

5. Prepare pasta according to the instructions on the packet.

6. Serve pasta with Bolognese sauce.

2. SHRIMP SOUP

Cal.: 127 | Fat: 8g | Protein: 23g

Preparation Time: 10 minutes
Cooking Time: 60 minutes
Servings: 1

Ingredients

1 pound shrimps
1 onion
2 carrots
1 bell pepper
1 yellow zucchini
3 garlic cloves
3 celery stalks
2 teaspoon chili powder
1 tablespoon olive oil
1 cup chicken broth
1 cup tomato juice
½ cup corn kernels
Salt, pepper, oregano as per taste

Directions

1. Heat oil in a pan and cook all the vegetables for 3 minutes. Add all the spices, broth and tomatoes. Simmer for 20 minutes.

2. Preheat the Sous Vide machine to 195°F/91°C.

3. Take the shrimps in a Ziploc bag and apply a vacuum to remove the air.

4. Place this bag in the water bath for 30 minutes.

5. The shrimps should turn pink.

6. Add the shrimps to the above pan and cook for 2 minutes.

7. Garnish with the lime wheels and serve hot.

3. OMELET WITH PARMESAN

Cal.: 303 | Fat: 17.39g | Protein: 21.85g

Preparation Time: 3 minutes
Cooking Time: 20 minutes
Servings: 1

Ingredients

2 large eggs
1 Tbsp. butter, diced
1 Tbsp. Parmesan cheese, finely grated
A pinch of salt and pepper
For Servings:
Fresh parsley, chopped
A pinch of basil

Directions

1. Preheat a water bath to 73°C/164°F.

2. In a large bowl, crack the eggs and whisk quickly. When they are well mixed, add butter, Parmesan, salt and pepper. Stir well.

3. Pour the mixture into a medium vacuum pouch and seal.

4. Put the bag in a water bath. Cook for 10 minutes.

5. After 10 minutes remove the bag from the bath and shake it well. That way, the eggs will start to get that "omelet look."

6. Put the bag back in the bath and cook for another 10 minutes.

7. When the eggs are finally cooked, transfer them to a plate.

8. Add a dash of basil and parsley and serve.

Photo by Saveurs Secretes from Pexels

4. CHOCOLATE CHIP COOKIES

Cal.: 199 | Fat: 9g | Protein: 22g

Preparation Time: 9 minutes
Cooking Time: 4 hours 30 minutes
Servings: 24

Ingredients

1 tsp. baking powder
1 cup all-purpose flour
6 tbsp. unsalted butter, at room temperature
¼ tsp. salt
1 large egg
2/3 cup packed dark brown sugar
1 cup chocolate chip cookies
2 tsp. vanilla extract

Directions

1. Preheat the Sous Vide machine to 195°F/91°C. Prepare 5 ½-pint canning jars and grease the insides with butter or spray with cooking spray.

2. Whisk together the salt, baking powder and flour in a medium bowl. Set aside.

3. In another bowl, combine the sugar and butter. Using an electric mixer set on medium-high speed,

beat the mixture for 3–5 minutes or until fluffy and light.

4. Add in the egg and beat until combined. Then, add in the vanilla and beat again for 3 minutes or until the mixture is very fluffy and light.

5. Add in the flour mixture into the bowl with the egg mixture and fold gently until just combined. Add in the chocolate chips and fold until evenly distributed.

6. Divide the dough evenly between the greased jars. Grease your fingers and pat the dough to the bottom of the jars. Clean the tops and sides of the jars using a damp towel.

7. Cover the jars with the lids and seal as tight as you can with just using your fingers to allow some air to escape. Place the jars into the water bath. Cook in the cooker for 3 hours.

8. Once done, carefully remove the jars from the water bath. Set the jars on a wire rack. Remove the lids to let the cookies cool.

9. Once the cookies are cool, carefully run a knife along the sides of the jars to unmold. Place the cookies on a plate and refrigerate to chill for 1 hour.

10. To serve, take a sharp knife to slice each cookie to make ¼-inch thick pieces. Serve immediately.

5. LEMON CURD

Cal.: 66 | Fat: 1g | Protein: 4g

Preparation Time: 11 minutes
Cooking Time: 70 minutes
Servings: 4

Ingredients

½ cup white sugar
1/4 cup lemon juice
1 tbsp. lemon zest
4 tbsp. unsalted butter
1 ½ tbsp. gelatin
3 fresh eggs
1 tsp. ground cinnamon for sprinkling

Directions

1. Preheat the Sous Vide machine to 165°F/74°C.

2. Put the ingredients into the plastic bag; and seal it, removing the air.

3. Set the timer for 1 hour.

4. When the time is up, blend the mixture with an immersion blender.

5. Wait until it cools down and refrigerate in portions.

6. Serve sprinkled with cinnamon.

6. SWEET PLUMS

Cal.: 69 | Fat: 0.2g | Protein: 0.7g

Preparation Time: 20 minutes
Cooking Time: 1 hour
Servings: 6

Ingredients

6 red plums, halved and deseeded
2 tablespoons Tamarind liquid
1/4 teaspoon Chinese five spices
2 tablespoons sugar
1 tablespoon honey
Zest of ½ orange

Directions

1. Prepare and preheat the water bath at 154°F/67°C.

2. Add plums and all the ingredients to a zipper-lock bag.

3. Seal the zipper-lock bag using the water immersion method.

4. Place the sealed bag in the bath and cook for 1 hour.

5. Once done, transfer the plums to a plate.

6. Serve.

7. CREAMY TOMATO SOUP

Cal.: 362 | Fat: 26g | Protein: 12g

Preparation Time: 18 minutes
Cooking Time: 60 minutes
Servings: 2

Ingredients

¼ cup butter
3 tablespoons flour
2 ¼ cups milk
½ cup heavy cream
1 ½ cans whole or diced tomatoes, peeled
1 fresh onion, chopped
1 small green pepper, chopped
1 garlic clove, chopped
1 tablespoon dried basil leaves
A pinch of cayenne pepper
Tabasco sauce to taste
½ teaspoon salt or to taste
½ teaspoon black pepper powder or to taste

Directions

1. Place a saucepan over medium heat. Add half the butter. When the butter starts melting, add flour and sauté for a couple of minutes stirring constantly.

2. Slowly add milk and continue stirring until the mixture thickens.

3. Add cream and continue stirring. Do not boil. Remove from heat and keep aside.

4. Place another saucepan over medium heat. Add the remaining butter. When butter melts, add onions, garlic and green pepper and sauté until the onions are translucent. Add tomatoes and basil and simmer for a few minutes.

5. Lower heat and add the white sauce, cayenne pepper, Tabasco, salt and pepper.

6. Set your machine to 172-175°F/78-79°C.

7. Place all the vegetables into a ziplock or a vacuum-seal bag and remove all the air. Seal and Immerse the bag in the water bath and cook for 45 minutes.

8. When done, purée the soup. Serve hot.

8. OLIVES SQUASH

Cal.: 263 | Fat: 23g | Protein: 15g

Preparation Time: 9 minutes
Cooking Time: 50 minutes
Servings: 4

Ingredients

1 tablespoon butter, melted
1 butternut squash, peeled and cubed
4 eggs, whisked
1 cup black olives, pitted and cubed
Salt and black pepper to the taste
½ cup tomatoes, chopped
2 garlic cloves, minced
½ teaspoon Italian seasoning
3 ounces Italian salami, chopped
1 tablespoon oregano, chopped

Directions

1. Prepare your sous-vide water bath to a temperature of 170°F/76°C.

2. Get a cooking pouch and add the eggs and the other ingredients listed above.

3. Shake the pouch to combine thoroughly, then

vacuum seal it.

4. Immerse the pouch in the water bath and cook for 40 minutes.

5. Remove the pouch once done and transfer the contents to a serving platter.

6. Serve and enjoy!

9. MUSHROOMS

Cal.: 429 | Fat: 34g | Protein: 18g

Preparation Time: 9 minutes
Cooking Time: 30 minutes
Servings: 8

Ingredients

2 pounds mushrooms of your choice
4 tablespoons extra-virgin olive oil
4 teaspoons minced fresh thyme
1 teaspoon salt or to taste
1 teaspoon freshly ground pepper, or to taste
4 tablespoons soy sauce
2 tablespoons vinegar of your choice

Directions

1. Preheat the Sous Vide machine to 176°F/80°C.

2. Place mushrooms in a bowl. Add the rest of the ingredients and stir until well coated.

3. Transfer into a large vacuum-seal pouch or Ziploc bag.

4. Vacuum seal the pouch.

5. Immerse the pouch in the water bath. Set the timer for 30 minutes.

6. When the timer goes off, remove the pouch from the water bath. Set aside to cool.

7. Open the pouch and transfer into a bowl.

8. Serve right away.

10. HARD-BOILED EGGS

Cal.: 78 | Fat: 5.3g | Protein: 6.29g

Preparation Time: 13 minutes
Cooking Time: 70 minutes
Servings: 3

Ingredients

1 ice bath
3 large eggs

Directions

1. Set the temperature in the machine at 165°F/74°C.

2. Arrange the eggs in the cooker. Prepare for 1 hour.

3. Once the time has elapsed, place the eggs into an ice bath.

4. When cool, peel and enjoy salads as a meal or just a snack anytime.

11. BREAKFAST YOGURT

Cal.: 134 | Fat: 4g | Protein: 3g

Preparation Time: 10 minutes
Cooking Time: 3 hours 10 minutes
Servings: 6

Ingredients

1 qt. almond milk
½ cup coconut yogurt
½ tablespoon lime, zest and grated
½ tablespoon orange, zest and grated
½ tablespoon lemon, zest and grated

Directions

1. Warm up the milk and mix with the yogurt in a bowl.

2. Whisk and add the rest of the fixings.

3. Pour the mixture into canning jars. Add to a water bath with the cooker and cover the tops with some foil.

4. Cook for 3 hours at 113°F/45°C.

5. Serve and enjoy!

12. TANGY GARLIC CHILI TOFU

Cal.: 377 | Fat: 29.8g | Protein: 7g

Preparation Time: 11 minutes
Cooking Time: 4 hours
Servings: 2

Ingredients

1 block of super firm tofu
1/4 cup brown sugar
1/4 cup soy sauce
1/4 cup toasted sesame oil
2 tablespoons chili garlic paste

Directions

1. Preheat the water bath to 180°F/82°C.

2. Press out liquid from tofu.

3. Cut tofu into thick chunks, about 2 inches each.

4. Preheat a frying pan on medium, spray with non-stick cooking spray, and cook until golden on each side.

5. Mix soy sauce, brown sugar, toasted sesame oil, and chili garlic paste together until well-blended in a mixing bowl.

6. Toss tofu in sauce to coat well.

7. Transfer tofu and sauce to a bag and seal.

8. Immerse in the bath and cook for 4 hours.

9. Remove and serve immediately.

13. HANGER STEAK

Cal.: 577 | Fat: 32g | Protein: 50g

Preparation Time: 6 minutes
Cooking Time: 4 hours
Servings: 4

Ingredients

4 (8 oz.) pieces of hanger steak
Kosher or truffle salt
Freshly ground black pepper
12 sprigs thyme
2 garlic cloves
2 shallots, peeled and thinly sliced
2 tbsp. high-smoke point oil

Directions

1. Preheat the Sous Vide machine to 130°F/54.5°C for a medium-rare steak. Change the temperature to 10°F in either direction to adjust wellness.

2. Season the steak with salt and pepper to taste.

3. Place the steak in the bag you're going to use to sous along with the sprigs of thyme, garlic and shallots. Divide the herbs, garlic, and shallots among the 4 steaks. Place thyme sprigs, and shallots slices on

both sides, and seal the bag.

4. Place the bag in your preheated water and set the timer for 4 hours.

5. When the steak is ready, allow it to rest for a few minutes.

6. While it's resting, heat a skittle (ideally cast-iron) on high heat. When it gets really hot, pour in the oil and put in the steak. Let the steak sear for 1 minute per side. Should form a nice crust on both sides.

7. Serve immediately.

14. AMAZING CHICKEN

Cal.: 198 | Fat: 10.4g | Protein: 20.6g

Preparation Time: 15 minutes
Cooking Time: 1 hour
Servings: 2

Ingredients

2 (6-ounce) skinless, boneless chicken breasts
Salt and freshly ground black pepper, to taste
2 thin prosciutto slices
1 tbsp. extra-virgin olive oil

Directions

1. Fill and preheat the bath to 145°F/63°C.

2. Cut each breast in half lengthwise and season with salt and pepper evenly.

3. Arrange a plastic wrap onto a cutting board.

4. Place 1 slice of prosciutto in the center of the plastic wrap.

5. Place 2 chicken strips side-by-side in the center of the prosciutto to form an even rectangle.

6. Roll prosciutto around the chicken to form a cylinder.

7. Wrap tightly in the plastic wrap and with butcher's twine, tie off the ends.

8. Repeat with remaining prosciutto and chicken.

9. In a cooking pouch, place the chicken cylinders.

10. Seal the pouch tightly after squeezing out the excess air.

11. Place the pouch in the bath and cook for about 1 hour.

12. Remove the pouch from the bath.

13. Remove the chicken cylinders from the pouch and discard the cooking liquid.

14. With paper towels, gently pat dry the chicken cylinders and season with salt and pepper.

15. In a large non-stick skillet, heat the oil on medium-high heat and sear the chicken cylinders till golden brown from all sides.

16. With a sharp knife, cut the roll into desired slices and serve.

15. SIMPLE RACK OF LAMB

Cal.: 494 | Fat: 32.8g | Protein: 46.2g

Preparation Time: 5 minutes
Cooking Time: 2 hours
Servings: 4

Photo by Chevanon Photography from Pexels

Ingredients

2 lbs. rack of lamb
2 tbsp. butter
2 tbsp. canola oil
Black pepper
Salt

Directions

1. Preheat the Sous Vide machine to 140°F/60°C.

2. Season lamb with pepper and salt and place in a large Ziploc bag.

3. Remove all air from the bag before sealing.

4. Place the bag in a hot water bath and cook for 2 hours.

5. Remove lamb from the bag and pat dry with paper towels.

6. Heat canola oil in a pan over medium heat.

7. Spread butter over lamb and sear lamb in hot oil until lightly brown.

8. Serve and enjoy!

16. PORK CARNITAS

Cal.: 729 | Fat: 51g | Protein: 55g

Preparation Time: 10 minutes
Cooking Time: 20 hours 10 minutes
Servings: 12

Ingredients

6 lb. pork shoulder
2 tbsp. anise
2 bay leaves
2 cinnamon sticks
3 tbsp. garlic, minced
4 bacon slices
1/3 cup brown sugar
2 orange juices
1 onion, chopped
1 tbsp. sea salt

Directions

1. Preheat the Sous Vide machine to 175°F/79°C.

2. In a small bowl, mix together anise, sugar, salt, garlic and orange juice.

3. Place pork into the Ziploc bag then pours orange juice mixture over pork.

4. Add cinnamon, bay leaves, bacon and onions into the bag.

5. Seal the bag and place into the hot water bath and cook for 20 hours.

6. Heat a large pan over medium-high heat.

7. Remove pork from bag and place on pan and shred using a fork.

8. Cook shredded pork until crispy.

9. Serve and enjoy!

Photo: "001 Tacos de carnitas, carne asada y al pastor.jpg" by Larry Miller

17. SPEEDY POACHED TOMATOES

Cal.: 180 | Fat: 16g | Protein: 34g

Preparation Time: 5 minutes
Cooking Time: 30 minutes
Servings: 3

Ingredients

4 cups Cherry Tomatoes
5 tbsp. Olive Oil
½ tbsp. Fresh Rosemary Leaves, minced
½ tbsp. Fresh Thyme Leaves, minced
Salt to taste
Pepper to taste

Directions

1. Make a water bath, place the machine in it, and set to 131°F/55°C.

2. Divide the listed ingredients into 2 vacuum-sealable bags, season with salt and pepper.

3. Release air by the water displacement method and seal the bags.

4. Immerse them in the water bath and set the timer to cook for 30 minutes.

5. Once the timer has stopped, remove the bag and unseal it.

6. Transfer the tomatoes with the juices into a bowl. Serve as a side dish.

18. BUFFALO CHICKEN WINGS

Cal.: 344 | Fat: 21g | Protein: 19g

Preparation Time: 11 minutes
Cooking Time: 30 minutes
Servings: 4

Ingredients

2 pounds whole chicken wings
½ cup butter
1 cup hot sauce (add another ½ cup if you like it hot)
1 teaspoon Worcestershire sauce
1 teaspoon garlic salt
1 teaspoon freshly ground black pepper.
½ cup all-purpose flour

Directions

1. Cut the chicken wings into 3 pieces. Keep the drumettes and wingettes (flats) but throw away the wing tips.

2. Fill the water bath with water. Set your machine temperature to 176°F/80°C.

3. Place the chicken wing pieces in a food-safe bag and vacuum seal the bag. Make sure they are lined up side by side and not stacked or piled. Use

multiple bags if necessary.

4. Place the chicken wings in the water bath and cook for 3 hours.

5. To make the buffalo sauce, melt the butter in a medium saucepan over medium heat. Add all the remaining ingredients, except the flour, and simmer for about 10 minutes, stirring often.

6. Prepare a Dutch oven or deep fryer with oil; preheat oil to 350°F.

7. Remove the chicken wings from the bag and pat dry with a paper towel.

8. Dredge the wings in flour. Shake off excess flour and deep-fry the chicken in 350°F oil for about 8–10 minutes.

9. Place the wings on paper towels to remove the excess oil and then toss them with buffalo sauce.

19. SZECHUAN BROCCOLI

Cal.: 414 | Fat: 36g | Protein: 19g

Preparation Time: 19 minutes
Cooking Time: 2 hours
Servings: 4

Ingredients

3 cups small broccoli florets
2 tablespoons olive oil
3 garlic cloves, minced
1 teaspoon grated fresh ginger root
3 tablespoons soy sauce
2 tablespoons rice vinegar
2 tablespoons granulated sugar
2 tablespoons ketchup
½ teaspoon dried red pepper flakes
2 tablespoons toasted sesame seeds

Directions

1. Fill the water bath with water. Set your machine temperature to 183°F/83°C.

2. Place the broccoli in a large food-safe bag and vacuum seal the bag. Make sure the broccoli is placed side by side and not stacked. Use multiple bags if necessary.

3. Place the bag in the water bath and cook for 1-1½ hours.

4. Heat the oil in a medium saucepan over medium heat. Add the garlic and ginger and cook for 2–3 minutes. Add the soy sauce, rice vinegar, sugar, ketchup and red pepper flakes. Let the sauce simmer for 7–9 minutes. It should thicken slightly.

5. Remove the bag from the water bath. Place the broccoli in a medium bowl and toss with the Szechuan sauce and toasted sesame seeds.

20. MASHED POTATOES

Cal.: 494 | Fat: 20g | Protein: 13g

Preparation Time: 19 minutes
Cooking Time: 2 hours
Servings: 4

Ingredients

2 pounds potatoes (white, Yukon Gold, or other), peeled and cut into 1" chunks
1/4 cup butter
1/4 cup heavy cream
½ cup whole milk
½ teaspoon sea salt
½ teaspoon freshly ground black pepper

Directions

1. Fill the water bath with water. Set your machine temperature to 183°F/84°C.

2. Place the chopped potatoes and butter in a food-safe bag and vacuum seal the bag. Make sure the potatoes are lined up side by side and not stacked or piled. Use multiple bags if necessary.

3. Place the potatoes in the water bath and cook for 1 ½-2 hours.

4. Drain the potatoes in a large bowl. Add the heavy cream, milk, salt and pepper. Mash the potatoes with a potato masher or a hand blender.

21. SCALLOPS WITH BROWN BUTTER

Cal.: 208 | Fat: 12.4g | Protein: 20.3g

Preparation Time: 6 minutes
Cooking Time: 36 minutes
Servings: 2

Ingredients

16 oz. scallops
4 tsp. brown butter
Salt and pepper

Directions

1. Preheat the Sous Vide machine to 140°F/60°C. Use a paper towel to gently dry the scallops.

2. Place the scallops in the bag with 2 tsp. brown butter and salt and pepper to taste.

3. Place the bag or bags in your preheated container and set your timer to 35 minutes.

4. Heat the remaining brown butter in a skillet on high heat.

5. When the scallops are cooked, take them out of the bag and place them in the skillet. Sear them for 30 seconds a side. They should have a golden color on both sides when seared.

6. Serve with your favorite side.

22. SWORDFISH

Cal.: 361 | Fat: 38g | Protein: 18g

Preparation Time: 8 minutes
Cooking Time: 50 minutes
Servings: 2

Ingredients

2 (6-ounce) swordfish steaks
2 tbsp. extra virgin olive oil
Zest and juice of 2 lemons
4 sprigs fresh thyme
Kosher salt and freshly ground black pepper to taste

Directions

1. Preheat the water bath to 130°F /55°C.

2. Season the swordfish with salt and pepper to taste.

3. Place in a large vacuum seal bag with olive oil, lemon zest, lemon juice and thyme.

4. Seal the bag using the moist setting.

5. Place in the water bath and cook for 30 minutes, or up to 45 minutes.

6. When it is finished cooking, remove the bag from the water bath.

7. Carefully remove the swordfish from the bag and pat dry with paper towels.

8. Reserve cooking liquid.

9. Heat a skillet to high heat and then sear the swordfish for 1 to 2 minutes on each side.

10. Transfer to a plate and let rest for 5 minutes.

11. Divide the swordfish between two serving plates and drizzle with some of the cooking liquid from the bag.

12. Serve.

23. PERSIMMON BUTTER TOASTS

Cal.: 129 | Fat: 9g | Protein: 4g

Preparation Time: 10 minutes
Cooking Time: 3 hours 50 minutes
Servings: 6

Ingredients

2 teaspoon orange juice
1 oz. French toasts
3 tablespoon sugar
½ teaspoon vanilla extract
¼ teaspoon salt
4 persimmon
½ teaspoon ground cinnamon

Directions

1. Add the chopped persimmons, vanilla extract, salt, orange juice and sugar in a Ziploc bag.

2. Remove the excess and seal the bag.

3. Turn the temperature to 154°F/67°C.

4. Immerse the bag into the preheated water bath.

5. Cook for 3 hours 50 minutes.

6. Remove the Ziploc bag from the water bath. Blend the Persimmons in a food blender until the mixture becomes smooth.

7. Remove the persimmon mixture from the blender and pour it over the French toast.

8. Serve and enjoy!

24. TENDER PORK CHOPS

Cal.: 378 | Fat: 32g | Protein: 18g

Preparation Time: 5 minutes
Cooking Time: 2 hours
Servings: 2

Ingredients

2 pork chops
1 tbsp. canola oil
1 tbsp. butter
4 garlic cloves
Rosemary
Thyme
Pepper
Salt

Directions

1. Preheat the Sous Vide machine to 140°F/60°C.

2. Season the pork with pepper and salt. Place pork chops into the Ziploc bag.

3. Remove all the air from the bag before sealing. Place the bag into the hot water bath and cook for 2 hours.

4. Remove pork from the bag and pat dry with a paper towel.

5. Heat oil and butter in a pan over high heat with rosemary, thyme, and garlic.

6. Place pork chops in a pan, sear until lightly brown, about 1 minute on each side.

7. Serve and enjoy!

25. HOLIDAY CRANBERRY SAUCE

Cal.: 102 | Fat: 0.2g | Protein: 3g

Preparation Time: 3 minutes
Cooking Time: 2 hours
Servings: 8

Ingredients

1 package frozen cranberries (or fresh)
1–2 tablespoons raw honey
1 cinnamon stick
2 fresh cloves
1 orange, sliced thin
½ tablespoon cinnamon
½ teaspoon nutmeg

Directions

1. Preheat the water bath to 185°F/85°C.

2. Place cranberries in a sealed bag along with the remaining ingredients and cook for about 2 hours.

3. Remove and transfer to an ice bath for 5-10 minutes.

4. Serve with your favorite meals; alternatively, you can refrigerate for up to 14 days.

26. JUICY BEER-INFUSED SAUSAGES

Cal.: 125 | Fat: 9.5g | Protein: 4.8g

Preparation Time: 21 minutes
Cooking Time: 4 hours
Servings: 8

Ingredients

3 lbs. natural-casing raw bratwurst sausage links
6 ounces craft beer
Dijon mustard
Sliced tomatoes
Sliced pickles
Chopped onions
Buns

Directions

1. Preheat the water bath to 160°F/71°C.

2. Add sausages to a vacuum bag in a single layer.

3. Add beer to the bag.

4. Seal the bag, but not airtight, so the sausages are not squeezed.

5. Add sausages to a water bath and cook for 4 hours.

6. Remove sausages from bags and discard beer.

7. Dry sausages carefully on a paper towel-lined plate.

8. Here, you can grill for 3 minutes each to sear or serve immediately on buns with your favorite toppings.

27. CHICKEN AND VEGETABLE SOUP

Cal.: 369 | Fat: 26g | Protein: 14g

Preparation Time: 12 minutes
Cooking Time: 68 minutes
Servings: 2

Ingredients

½ cup zucchini, diced
½ cup red bell pepper, diced
½ cup cauliflower, chopped
3 baby carrots, chopped
1 medium onion, chopped
2 cups fresh spinach leaves
½ teaspoon garlic powder or to taste
½ teaspoon onion powder
Sea salt to taste
Black pepper powder to taste
Cayenne pepper to taste
1 cup chicken, diced, cooked
½ tablespoon olive oil
2 cups chicken broth

Directions

1. Preheat the Sous Vide machine to 140°F/60°C.

2. Season the pork with pepper and salt. Place pork chops into the Ziploc bag.

3. Remove all the air from the bag before sealing. Place the bag into the hot water bath and cook for 2 hours.

4. Remove pork from the bag and pat dry with a paper towel. Heat oil and butter in a pan over high heat with rosemary, thyme, and garlic.

5. Place pork chops in a pan, sear until lightly brown, about 1 minute on each side.

6. Serve and enjoy!

28. CREAMY CAULIFLOWER BROCCOLI SOUP

Cal.: 102 | Fat: 5.9g | Protein: 3g

Preparation Time: 5 minutes
Cooking Time: 2 hours 3 minutes
Servings: 2

Ingredients

1 medium cauliflower, cut into small florets
½ lb. Broccoli, cut into small florets
1 Green Bell Pepper, chopped
1 medium White Onion, diced
1 tsp. Olive Oil
1 garlic clove, crushed
½ cup Vegetable Stock
½ cup Skimmed Milk

Directions

1. Make a water bath, place the machine in it, and set it to 185°F/85°C.

2. Place the cauliflower, broccoli, bell pepper and white onion in a vacuum-sealable bag and pour olive oil into it.

3. Release air by the water displacement method and

seal the bag. Immerse the bag in the water bath. Set the timer for 50 minutes and cook.

4. Once the timer has stopped, remove the bag and unseal it. Transfer the vegetables to a blender, add garlic and milk, and purée to smooth.

5. Place a pan over medium heat, add the vegetable purée and vegetable stock and simmer for 3 minutes. Season with salt and pepper. Serve warm as a side dish.

29. TERIYAKI SALMON

Cal.: 291 | Fat: 12g | Protein: 33g

Preparation Time: 10 minutes
Cooking Time: 2 hours 15 minutes
Servings: 2

Ingredients

½ cup plus 1 teaspoon teriyaki sauce
2 (5 oz.) skinless salmon fillets
4 oz. Chinese egg noodles
1 tablespoon sesame oil
2 teaspoons soy sauce
2 teaspoons thinly sliced scallions, plus 4 (1-inch pieces) scallion greens, for serving
1-inch fresh ginger, peeled and sliced into thin strips
4 oz. lettuce, chopped
1/8 small red onion, thinly sliced
1 tablespoon Japanese roasted sesame dressing
1 tablespoon sesame seeds, toasted

Directions

1. Divide ½ cup teriyaki sauce between 2 Ziploc bags.

2. Place 1 salmon fillet in each bag and seal bags using the water immersion method.

3. Do not place salmon fillets, but place aside to marinate at room temperature for 15 minutes.

4. Meanwhile, preheat the Sous Vide machine to 131°F/55°C. Place the bags in a water bath and cook for 15 minutes.

5. While salmon is cooking, prepare egg noodles according to package instructions.

6. Drain well, return to the cooking pot and stir in sesame oil and soy sauce, reserving one teaspoon

7. Divide pasta between serving plates.

8. Prepare the dipping sauce; combine scallions, ginger, remaining teriyaki sauce and one teaspoon soy sauce.

9. Also, prepare the salad by combining lettuce and onion with one tablespoon of roasted sesame dressing.

10. When the timer goes off, remove salmon from the water bath, reserving cooking liquid.

11. Top the pasta with salmon fillets and drizzle all with reserved cooking liquid.

12. Garnish salmon with sesame seeds and serve with prepared salad and dipping sauce.

30. STRAWBERRIES

Cal.: 80 | Fat: 12g | Protein: 0.6g

Preparation Time: 11 minutes
Cooking Time: 16 minutes
Servings: 4

Ingredients

12 oz. strawberries trimmed
2 tbsp. champagne
2 tsp. sugar

Directions

1. Preheat your Sous Vide Machine to 185°F/85°C.

2. Place all the ingredients in a bag and place the bag in the preheated container and set your timer for 15 minutes.

3. Meanwhile, prepare an ice bath. When the strawberries are cooked, put them directly in the ice bath until they're cold.

Photo by Fidel Fernando on Unsplash

31. MIXED VEGETABLES

Cal.: 244 | Fat: 13.2g | Protein: 3.5g

Preparation Time: 15 minutes
Cooking Time: 3 hours
Servings: 4

Photo by Christina Rumpf on Unsplash

Ingredients

1 potato, peeled and diced
1 butternut squash, peeled and diced
½ cauliflower head, diced into florets
6 carrots, peeled and diced
1 parsnip, peeled and diced
½ red onion, peeled and diced
4 garlic cloves, crushed
4 sprigs of fresh rosemary
2 tablespoons olive oil
Salt and black pepper, to taste
2 tablespoons butter

Directions

1. Prepare and preheat the water bath at 185°F/85°C.

2. Add vegetables and all the ingredients to a zipper-lock bag.

3. Seal the zipper-lock bag using the water immersion method.

4. Place the sealed bag in the bath and cook for 3 hours.

5. Once done, transfer the vegetables along with the sauce to a plate.

6. Serve.

32. SWEET POTATO FRIES

Cal.: 134 | Fat: 8g | Protein: 2g

Preparation Time: 9 minutes
Cooking Time: 75 minutes
Servings: 4

Ingredients

2 tablespoons canola oil
1 cup water
1 ½ pounds sweet potatoes, peeled and cut into sticks
1/4 teaspoon ground allspice
1 tablespoon sea salt

Directions

1. Prepare your sous-vide water bath to a temperature of 183°F/84°C.

2. In a cooking pouch, add the potatoes, salt and water and vacuum seal it. Immerse the pouch into the preheated water bath and let it cook for 1 hour.

3. Once done, remove the pouch from the water bath and remove the potatoes.

4. Pat dry the potatoes and toss in a bowl with canola oil.

5. Place the parchment paper on a baking sheet lined with parchment.

6. Preheat the oven to 400°F/205°C and bake for 11 minutes until crispy.

7. Serve and enjoy with a dipping sauce of your choice.

33. SCRAMBLED EGGS

Cal.: 384 | Fat: 28g | Protein: 13g

Preparation Time: 9 minutes
Cooking Time: 12 minutes
Servings: 4

Image by Markéta Machová from Pixabay

Ingredients

8 large eggs
Freshly ground pepper to taste
Salt to taste
Aleppo pepper to taste (optional)

Directions

1. Preheat the Sous Vide machine to 165°F/74°C.

2. Add eggs, salt, and pepper into a bowl and whisk well. Pour into a large silicone bag and vacuum seal the pouch.

3. Immerse the pouch in the water bath and adjust the timer for 10 minutes.

4. Remove the pouch from the water bath and place the pouch between your palms. Press it and shake it.

5. Place it back in the water bath. Set the timer for 12 minutes.

6. When the timer goes off, remove the pouch from the water bath.

7. Open the pouch and divide into 4 plates.

8. Garnish with Aleppo pepper. Serve immediately.

34. HARISSA CHICKEN

Cal.: 643 | Fat: 50g | Protein: 43.5g

Preparation Time: 31 minutes
Cooking Time: 2 hours
Servings: 2

Ingredients

2 boneless, skinless chicken breasts
1 tablespoon harissa, powdered; or ½ tablespoon harissa paste
½ teaspoon cayenne pepper
2 garlic cloves, minced
Sea salt, to taste
1 preserved lemon, chopped
4 tablespoons olive oil, divided

Directions

1. Add all ingredients to a resealable bag and marinate for 30 minutes. Use only half the olive oil.

2. Preheat the water bath to 141°F/61°C.

3. Seal the bag and add chicken to the water bath and cook for 2 hours.

4. Heat remaining olive oil in a frying pan on medium-high.

5. Remove chicken from the water bath and sear on both sides for 2 minutes.

6. Serve with juices over couscous and enjoy!

35. APPLE BUTTERNUT SQUASH SOUP

Cal.: 226 | Fat: 7.3g | Protein: 3.6g

Preparation Time: 11 minutes
Cooking Time: 2 hours
Servings: 4

Ingredients

1 medium butternut squash,
1 large tart apple
½ yellow onion
1 teaspoon sea salt
3/4 cup light cream

Directions

1. Preheat your bath to 185°F/85°C. Core and slice the apple, peel and slice the butternut squash, slice the onion.

2. Place the butternut squash, apple and onion in a bag. Seal and place the bag in your preheated container and set your timer for 2 hours.

3. Once cooked, place the ingredients in a blender and blend until smooth. Add the remaining ingredients and purée again.

36. WALNUT COATED HALIBUT

Cal.: 453 | Fat: 29g | Protein: 10g

Preparation Time: 15 minutes
Cooking Time: 25 minutes
Servings: 4

Ingredients

1 egg white
1 cup walnut
4 halibut fillets
2 tablespoons all-purpose flour
3 oranges
½ tablespoon red onion
2 tablespoon cilantro
1 jalapeno pepper
1 teaspoon vinegar
Salt, pepper, mashed potatoes

Directions

1. Add flour, salt and pepper in one bowl.

2. Beat the egg with water in another bowl.

3. Take crushed walnut in the third bowl.

4. Coat the fish with flour mixture, dip it in egg mixture and coat it with the crushed walnut.

5. Preheat the Sous Vide machine to 195°F/91°C.

6. Place these fish pieces in a large Ziploc bag in a side by side manner.

7. Apply vacuum to remove the air.

8. Place this bag in the water bath for 30 minutes.

9. In a bowl toss onion, oranges, cilantro, vinegar and jalapeno.

10. Serve the above salad with the cooked fish.

37. SPICY BUTTER POACHED ASPARAGUS

Cal.: 78 | Fat: 9g | Protein: 0.2g

Preparation Time: 10 minutes
Cooking Time: 10-12 minutes
Servings: 4

Ingredients

1 bunch of asparagus, trimmed
3 tablespoons unsalted butter
½ teaspoon cayenne pepper
Pinch of salt

Directions

1. Set your immersion circulator for 185°F/85°C.

2. Trim the bottoms of the asparagus and place them flat in a vacuum-sealed bag.

3. Melt the butter and add the cayenne pepper. Drizzle the spiced butter over the asparagus and use a vacuum sealer to seal the bag.

4. When the water bath has reached the proper temperature, place the bag in the water and cook for 10 to 12 minutes.

5. Remove the bag from the water and sprinkle a pinch of salt on the asparagus before serving.

38. FUDGY BROWNIES

Cal.: 173 | Fat: 6g | Protein: 22g

Preparation Time: 13 minutes
Cooking Time: 3 hours 20 minutes
Servings: 16

Ingredients

3 ounces of bittersweet chocolate, chopped
1 stick of unsalted butter
2 large eggs
¾ cup plus 2 tablespoons of granulated sugar
2/3 cup all-purpose flour
1 tsp. vanilla extract
¼ tsp. salt

Directions

1. Preheat the Sous Vide machine to 195°F/91°C.

2. Prepare 4 ½-pint canning jars and grease the insides with butter or spray with cooking spray.

3. Set a double boiler by placing a large bowl over a medium saucepan with 1 inch of water. Set over medium heat and bring the water to a simmer.

4. Once the water is simmering, place the chocolate

and butter into the bowl. Stir frequently to mix the melting butter and chocolate.

5. Once completely melted, place the bowl on the counter and place a towel underneath. Add in the sugar and whisk until combined. Whisk in the eggs, one at a time, until the mixture is smooth. Add in the vanilla and whisk again.

6. Add in the salt and flour and gently fold until just combined.

7. Divide the batter equally among the prepared jars, filling each jar about halfway full. Clean the tops and sides of the jars using a damp towel. Tap the jars to remove the excess bubbles.

8. Cover the jars with the lids and screw only as tight as you can with just using your fingertips.

9. Place the jars into the water bath. Cook in the cooker for 3 hours.

10. Once done, carefully remove the jars from the cooker and set on a cooling rack. Remove the lids to let the brownies cool.

11. Once the brownies have completely cooled down, run a knife around the edges of the jars to unmold. Divide each brownie into 4 horizontal slices to make individual servings. Serve immediately.

39. COLD PEA AND YOGURT SOUP

Cal.: 135 | Fat: 7g | Protein: 1g

Preparation Time: 10 minutes
Cooking Time: 1 hour
Servings: 4

Ingredients

1 onion, chopped
2 garlic cloves, minced
1 carrot, peeled and grated
1 ½ cups frozen peas
2 cups vegetable stock
Salt and pepper to taste
Greek yogurt for serving
Chopped dill or cilantro for serving

Directions

1. Preheat the Sous Vide machine to 183°F/84°C.

2. Place the onion, garlic and carrot into the vacuum bag, and seal it, removing the air.

3. Set the cooking time for 50 minutes.

4. Blend the cooked vegetable with the stock using an immersion blender, and salt and pepper to taste.

5. Serve refrigerated with yogurt and chopped dill or cilantro.

40. POWER GREEN SOUP

Cal.: 153 | Fat: 1g | Protein: 6g

Preparation Time: 10 minutes
Cooking Time: 40 minutes
Servings: 3

Ingredients

4 cups vegetable stock
1 tbsp. olive oil
1 garlic clove, crushed
1-inch ginger, sliced
1 tsp. coriander powder
1 large zucchini, diced
3 cups kale
2 cups broccoli, cut into florets
1 lime, juiced and zest

Directions

1. Make a water bath, place a cooker in it, and set it at 185°F/85°C. Place the broccoli, zucchini, kale and parsley in a vacuum-sealable bag.

2. Release air by the water displacement method, seal and Immerse the bag in the water bath. Set the timer for 30 minutes.

3. Once the timer has stopped, remove and unseal the bag. Add the steamed ingredients to a blender with garlic and ginger. Purée to smooth.

4. Pour the green purée into a pot and add the remaining listed ingredients.

5. Put the pot over medium heat and simmer for 10 minutes. Serve as a light dish.

41. BACON BRUSSELS SPROUTS

Cal.: 230 | Fat: 4g | Protein: 20.2g

Preparation Time: 20 minutes
Cooking Time: 65 minutes
Servings: 4

Ingredients

Brussels sprouts (1 lb., trimmed, halved)
2 tbsp. butter
2 ounces thick-cut bacon, fried and chopped
2 garlic cloves, minced
¼ tsp. salt
¼ tsp. pepper

Directions

1. Preheat the water bath to 183°F/84°C. Combine all your ingredients in a large Ziploc bag.

2. Seal and place in a water bath. Cook for 1 hour. Meanwhile, preheat the oven to 400°F/205°C. After 1 hour has passed, transfer Brussels sprouts onto a lined baking tray.

3. Set to bake until nicely roasted (about 5 minutes). Enjoy!

42. TROUT

Cal.: 459 | Fat: 49g | Protein: 31g

Preparation Time: 7 minutes
Cooking Time: 53 minutes
Servings: 4

Ingredients

2 trout portions, each weighing 150g
Pinch of sea salt
Sprigs of thyme
4-6 fresh basil leaves
1 tbsp. olive oil

Directions

1. Preheat the water bath to 113°F /45°C. Salt the trout portions. Lay both trout pieces flat inside a vacuum bag. Add the olive oil, thyme, and basil.

2. Seal the bag and place in the water bath. Cook for 45 minutes.

3. Remove trout from the vacuum bag and pat dry. Heat a dash of oil in a skillet on high heat.

4. When the oil is hot, sear the skin side of the trout until it turns golden brown and crispy. Serve.

43. FENNEL RISOTTO

Cal.: 136 | Fat: 9g | Protein: 4g

Preparation Time: 15 minutes
Cooking Time: 46 minutes
Servings: 4

Ingredients

1 cup Arborio rice
3 cups vegetable broth
1 glass white wine
1 tbsp. olive oil
Salt and pepper
4 fennel bulbs, trimmed cut in half
A little butter
Freshly grated Parmesan cheese, for serving

Directions

1. Preheat the Sous Vide machine to 183°F/83°C.

2. Place the first 5 ingredients in the bag you're going to use to sous and the fennel and a little butter in a separate bag, and seal them.

3. Place the bags in your preheated water and set the timer for 45 min.

4. Place the cooked risotto in 4 bowls and fluff it with a fork.

5. Mix in the cheese and fennel, and serve.

44. SESAME EGGPLANT

Cal.: 200 | Fat: 7.2g | Protein: 4.5g

Preparation Time: 20 minutes
Cooking Time: 3 hours 5 minutes
Servings: 2

Ingredients

1 eggplant, cut into ½-inch slices
1/4 cup Worcestershire sauce
2 tablespoons red wine
1 tablespoon soy sauce
1 tablespoon sugar
1 teaspoon sesame oil
Salt, to taste
2 tablespoons sesame seeds, toasted
2 tablespoons scallions, sliced

Directions

1. Prepare and preheat the water bath at 185°F/85°C.

2. Add sliced eggplant to a zipper-lock bag. Seal the zipper-lock bag using the water immersion method.

3. Place the sealed bag in the bath and cook for 3 hours. Once done, transfer the eggplant to a plate.

4. Mix the remaining sauce ingredients, except sesame seeds in a bowl and pour over the eggplant.

5. Spread the eggplant in a baking tray and broil for 5 minutes.

6. Garnish with sesame seeds.

7. Serve.

45. CRÈME BRULÉE WITH BLUEBERRIES

Cal.: 493 | Fat: 5g | Protein: 48g

Preparation Time: 9 minutes
Cooking Time: 2 hours 35 minutes
Servings: 4

Ingredients

2 cups heavy cream
4 egg yolks
¼ cup sugar
1 tsp. vanilla extract
Zest from 1 orange
1 cup fresh blueberries

Directions

1. Set your cooker to 180°F/82°C.

2. Whisk together all the ingredients and pour the mixture into 4 shallow jars.

3. Seal the jars and Immerse in the preheated water bath.

4. Cook for 30 minutes.

5. Once the timer has stopped, remove the jars and refrigerate for 2 hours.

6. Unseal the jars and sprinkle sugar on top of each custard.

7. Place under the broiler until they become caramelized.

8. Serve garnished with fresh blueberries

46. KALE CHEESE

Cal.: 79 | Fat: 6g | Protein: 7g

Preparation Time: 9 minutes
Cooking Time: 2 hours 50 minutes
Servings: 10

Photo by alleksana from Pexels

Ingredients

1 cup ale
4 ounces Colby cheese, shredded
1/4 cup Thai fish sauce
½ pound Cottage cheese
1 cup kale leaves, chopped
2 garlic cloves, smashed
1 sun-dried Thai chili, finely chopped
1 teaspoon mustard powder
Sea salt and ground black pepper, to taste

Directions

1. Preheat the container with water and set the temperature to 183°F/84°C.

2. In a Ziploc bag, add all the listed ingredients and seal it after removing the excess air.

3. Immerse the bag into the water bath and cook for 45 minutes.

4. Serve and enjoy with vegetable chips, tortilla chips, or breadsticks.

47. RED WINE POACHED PEARS

Cal.: 299 | Fat: 0.3g | Protein: 1g

Preparation Time: 9 minutes
Cooking Time: 2 hours 6 hours
Servings: 4

Ingredients

4 ripe Bosc pears
1 cup red wine
½ cup granulated sugar
1/4 cup sweet vermouth
1 tsp. salt
3 (3-inch pieces) orange zest
1 vanilla bean
Vanilla ice cream

Directions

1. Preheat your Sous Vide Machine to 175°F/79°C. Peel the pear and scrape the vanilla bean seeds.

2. Put everything, except the ice cream in a bag. Then, place the bag in the preheated container and set your timer for 1 hour.

3. When the pears are cooked, slice them up and core them. Reserve the juices from the bag.

4. Place the sliced pears in 4 bowls and add a scoop of ice cream. Top with the reserved juices and serve.

48. BUTTERED SPICED APPLES

Cal.: 229 | Fat: 12g | Protein: 0.9g

Preparation Time: 21 minutes
Cooking Time: 2 hours
Servings: 6

Ingredients

Zest and juice from 1 lemon
6 small apples
6 tbsp. unsalted butter
½ tsp. salt
½ tsp. ground cinnamon
1/4 tsp. ground nutmeg
1 heaping tsp. dark brown sugar
1 heaping tablespoon dark or golden raisins
Dollops of crème fraiche, whipped cream or ice cream

Directions

1. Preheat your Sous Vide Machine to 170°F/77°C. Peel and core the apples, soften the butter, and completely zest the lemon.

2. Coat the apples with lemon juice. Place the lemon zest in a bowl and combine with the cinnamon, sugar, nutmeg, raisins, butter and salt. Place an

equal amount of the mixture in the hollowed-out center of each apple.

3. Put 2 apples in each bag and set your timer for 2 hours.

4. Remove apples from the bag and serve immediately with cooking liquid.

Image by Cosmetically Corinne from Pixabay

49. BLUEBERRY JAM

Cal.: 50 | Fat: 0.6g | Protein: 0.2g

Preparation Time: 11 minutes
Cooking Time: 90 minutes
Servings: 10

Ingredients

2 cups blueberries
1 cup white sugar
2 tbsp. lemon juice

Directions

1. Preheat the water bath to 180°F/82°C.

2. Put the ingredients into the vacuum bag and seal it.

3. Cook for 1 hour 30 min in the water bath.

4. Serve over ice cream or cake, or store in the fridge in an airtight container.

50. ARTICHOKE

Cal.: 370 | Fat: 22g | Protein: 14g

Preparation Time: 15 minutes
Cooking Time: 30 minutes
Servings: 2

Ingredients

1 whole artichoke
2 tablespoons vegan butter
1 garlic clove, sautéed
1 teaspoon sea salt

Directions

1. Pre-heat your water bath by submerging the immersion circulator and set the temperature at 180°F/82°C.

2. Peel outer leaves and stems of the artichokes. Then cut up the artichokes in half from the bloom end to the stem end. Season it with salt and garlic. Add all the listed ingredients into a heavy-duty resealable zip bag.

3. Seal bag using the immersion method, Immerse it.

4. Cook for 30 minutes. Serve and enjoy!

TEMPERATURE CHARTS

🥩 MEAT	°F🌡 TEMPERATURE	⏱ TIME
Beef Steak, rare	129 °F	1 hour 30 min.
Beef Steak, medium-rare	136 °F	1 hour 30min.
Beef Steak, well done	158 °F	1 hour 30min.
Beef Roast, rare	133 °F	7 hours
Beef Roast, medium-rare	140 °F	6 hours
Beef Roast, well done	158 °F	5 hours
Beef Tough Cuts, rare	136 °F	24 hours
Beef Tough Cuts, medium-rare	149 °F	16 hours
Beef Tough Cuts, well done	185 °F	8 hours
Lamb Tenderloin, Rib eye, T-bone, Cutlets	134 °F	4 hours
Lamb Roast, Leg	134 °F	10 hours
Lamb Flank Steak, Brisket	134 °F	12 hours
Pork Chop, rare	136 °F	1 hour
Pork Chop, medium-rare	144 °F	1 hour
Pork Chop, well done	158 °F	1 hour
Pork Roast, rare	136 °F	3 hours

🥩 MEAT	°F TEMPERATURE	⏱ TIME
Pork Roast, medium-rare	144 °F	3 hours
Pork Roast, well done	158 °F	3 hours
Pork Tough Cuts, rare	144 °F	16 hours
Pork Tough Cuts, medium-rare	154 °F	12 hours
Pork Tough Cuts, well done	154 °F	8 hours
Pork Tenderloin	134 °F	1 hour 30min
Pork Baby Back Ribs	165 °F	6 hours
Pork Cutlets	134 °F	5 hours
Pork Spare Ribs	160 °F	12 hours
Pork Belly (quick)	185 °F	5 hours
Pork Belly (slow)	167 °F	24 hours

🐟 FISH AND SEAFOOD	°F TEMPERATURE	⏱ TIME
Fish, tender	104 °F	40 min.
Fish, tender and flaky	122 °F	40 min.
Fish, well done	140 °F	40 min.
Salmon, Tuna, Trout, Mackerel, Halibut, Snapper, Sole	126 °F	30 min.
Lobster	140 °F	50 min.
Scallops	140 °F	50 min.
Shrimp	140 °F	35 min.

🍗 POULTRY	°F🌡 TEMPERATURE	⏱ TIME
Chicken White Meat, super-supple	140 °F	2 hours
Chicken White Meat, tender and juicy	149 °F	1 hour
Chicken White Meat, well done	167 °F	1 hour
Chicken Breast, bone-in	146 °F	2 hours 30 min.
Chicken Breast, boneless	146 °F	1 hour
Turkey Breast, bone-in	146 °F	4 hours
Turkey Breast, boneless	146 °F	2 hours 30 min.
Duck Breast	134 °F	1 hour 30 min.
Chicken Dark Meat, tender	149 °F	1 hour 30 min.
Chicken Dark Meat, falling off the bone	167 °F	1 hour 30 min.
Chicken Leg or Thigh, bone-in	165 °F	4 hours
Chicken Thigh, boneless	165 °F	1 hour
Turkey Leg or Thigh	165 °F	2 hours
Duck Leg	165 °F	8 hours
Split Game Hen	150 °F	6 hours

🥕 VEGETABLES	°F 🌡 TEMPERA-TURE	⏱ TIME
Vegetables, root (carrots, potato, parsnips, beets, celery root, turnips)	183 °F	3 hours
Vegetables, tender (asparagus, broccoli, cauliflower, fennel, onions, pumpkin, eggplant, green beans, corn)	183 °F	1 hour
Vegetables, greens (kale, spinach, collard greens, Swiss chard)	183 °F	3 min.

🍎 FRUITS	°F 🌡 TEMPERA-TURE	⏱ TIME
Fruit, firm (apple, pear)	183 °F	45 min.
Fruit, for purée	185 °F	30 min.
Fruit, berries for topping desserts (blueberries, blackberries, raspberries, strawberries, cranberries)	154 °F	30 min.

WHAT TEMPERATURE SHOULD BE USED?

The rule of thumb is that the thicker the piece, the longer it should cook. Higher temperatures shorten the cooking time. Lower temperatures may take longer.

	TEMPERATURE	MIN COOKING TIME	MAX COOKING TIME
EGGS			
Soft Yolk	140°F (60°C)	1 hour	1 hour
Creamy Yolk	145°F (63°C)	¾ hour	1 hour
GREEN VEGETABLES			
Rare	183°F (84°C)	¼ hour	¾ hour
ROOTS			
Rare	183°F (84°C)	1 hour	3 hours
FRUITS			
Warm	154°F (68°C)	1¾ hour	2½ hour
Soft Fruits	185°F (85°C)	½ hour	1½ hour

	TEMPERATURE	MIN COOKING TIME	MAX COOKING TIME
CHICKEN			
Rare	140°F (60°C)	1 hour	3 hours
Medium	150°F (65°C)	1 hour	3 hours
Well Done	167°F (75°C)	1 hour	3 hours
BEEF STEAK			
Rare	130°F (54°C)	1½ hours	3 hours
Medium	140°F (60°C)	1½ hours	3 hours
Well Done	145°F (63°C)	1½ hours	3 hours
ROAST BEEF			
Rare	133°F (54°C)	7 hours	16 hours
Medium	140°F (60°C)	6 hours	14 hours
Well Done	158°F (70°C)	5 hours	11 hours
PORK CHOP BONE-IN			
Rare	136°F (58°C)	1 hour	4 hours
Medium	144°F (62°C)	1 hour	4 hours
Well Done	158°F (70°C)	1 hour	4 hours
PORK LOIN			
Rare	136°F (58°C)	3 hours	5½ hours
Medium	144°F (62°C)	3 hours	5 hours
Well Done	158°F (70°C)	3 hours	3½ hours
FISH			
Tender	104°F (40°C)	½ hour	½ hour
Medium	124°F (51°C)	½ hour	1 hour
Well Done	131°F (55°C)	½ hour	1½ hours

COOKING CONVERSION

TEMPERATURE CONVERSIONS	
CELSIUS	**FAHRENHEIT**
54.5°C	130°F
60.0°C	140°F
65.5°C	150°F
71.1°C	160°F
76.6°C	170°F
82.2°C	180°F
87.8°C	190°F
93.3°C	200°F
100°C	212°F

WEIGHT COVERSION	
½ oz.	15g
1 oz.	30g
2 oz.	60g
3 oz.	85g
4 oz.	110g
5 oz.	140g
6 oz.	170g
7 oz.	200g
8 oz.	225g
9 oz.	255g
10 oz.	280g
11 oz.	310g
12 oz.	340g
13 oz.	370g
14 oz.	400g
15 oz.	425g
1 lb.	450g

LIQUID VOLUME CONVERSION		
CUPS / TABLESPOONS	FL. OUNCES	MILLILITERS
1 cup	8 fl. Oz.	240 ml
¾ cup	6 fl. Oz.	180 ml
2/3 cup	5 fl. Oz.	150 ml
½ cup	4 fl. Oz.	120 ml
1/3 cup	2 ½ fl. Oz.	75 ml
¼ cup	2 fl. Oz.	60 ml
1/8 cup	1 fl. Oz.	30 ml
1 tablespoon	½ fl. Oz.	15 ml

TEASPOON (tsp.) / TABLESPOON (Tbsp.)	MILLILITERS
1 tsp.	5ml
2 tsp.	10ml
1 Tbsp.	15ml
2 Tbsp.	30ml
3 Tbsp.	45ml
4 Tbsp.	60ml
5 Tbsp.	75ml
6 Tbsp.	90ml
7 Tbsp.	105ml

LIQUID VOLUME MEASUREMENTS			
TABLE-SPOONS	TEASPOONS	FLUID OUNCES	CUPS
16	48	8 fl. Oz.	1
12	36	6 fl. Oz.	¾
8	24	4 fl. Oz.	½
5 ½	16	2 2/3 fl. Oz.	1/3
4	12	2 fl. Oz.	¼
1	3	0.5 fl. Oz.	1/16

RECIPE INDEX

Amazing Chicken 36
Apple Butternut Squash Soup 78
Artichoke 106
Bacon Brussels Sprouts 90
Blueberry Jam 104
Bolognese Sauce for Spaghetti 12
Breakfast Yogurt 31
Buffalo Chicken Wings 44
Buttered Spiced Apples 102
Chicken and Vegetable Soup 62
Chocolate Chip Cookies 18
Cold Pea and Yogurt Soup 86
Creamy Cauliflower Broccoli Soup 64
Creamy Tomato Soup 24
Crème Brulée with Blueberries 96
Fennel Risotto 92
Fudgy Brownies 84
Hanger Steak 34
Hard-Boiled Eggs 30
Harissa Chicken 76
Holiday Cranberry Sauce 58
Juicy Beer-Infused Sausages 60
Kale Cheese 98
Lemon Curd 20

Mashed Potatoes	48
Mixed Vegetables	70
Mushrooms	28
Olives Squash	26
Omelet With Parmesan	16
Persimmon Butter Toasts	54
Pork Carnitas	40
Power Green Soup	88
Red Wine Poached Pears	100
Scallops with Brown Butter	50
Scrambled Eggs	74
Sesame Eggplant	94
Shrimp Soup	14
Simple Rack of Lamb	38
Speedy Poached Tomatoes	42
Spicy Butter Poached Asparagus	82
Strawberries	68
Sweet Plums	22
Sweet Potato Fries	72
Swordfish	52
Szechuan Broccoli	46
Tangy Garlic Chili Tofu	32
Tender Pork Chops	56
Teriyaki Salmon	66
Trout	91
Walnut Coated Halibut	80

www.ingramcontent.com/pod-product-compliance
Lightning Source LLC
Chambersburg PA
CBHW070923080526
44589CB00013B/1407